CELEBRATIONS

William Plomer

CELEBRATIONS

JONATHAN CAPE
THIRTY BEDFORD SQUARE LONDON

821·08
PLO

Printed and bound in Great Britain
by Richard Clay (The Chaucer Press) Ltd, Bungay, Suffolk

CONTENTS

5

ACKNOWLEDGMENTS

Acknowledgments are due to the editors of the following periodicals, in which most of these poems first appeared, *London Magazine, Poetry Review, Listener, New Statesman, Sunday Times, Country Life, Outposts, Workshop, Wave, Contrast, Ophir, Sewanee Review, Harper's Bazaar, Journal of Creative Behavior.*

Thanks are offered to those who commissioned two of the poems for special occasions, *White Gloves* for the Camden Festival in 1970 and *The Planes of Bedford Square* for the Book Bang held there in 1971. The former, in an earlier version, was printed in *Twelve to Twelve*, edited by Jeni Couzyn and published by Poets Trust, the latter in *Responses*, published by the National Book League and the Poetry Society.

Anonyma has been printed in the P.E.N. anthology, *New Poems 1970–71*, edited by Alan Brownjohn, Seamus Heaney, and John Stallworthy, and published by Hutchinson.

[1]

A NOTE FROM A CELLO

[In the summer of 1969 the Maltings, the great
concert-hall near Aldeburgh, was destroyed by fire.
These lines were written to celebrate its restoration
in 1970.]

A blameless calm night, the people have gone.
Dark thickets of reeds feel a breath of disquiet:
Moorhens awake; fear saves the vole
About to be hooked by the soft-flying owl;
In the marshes of Snape a sluice and a pool
Make suddenly shapes of flame-coloured light.

A crackle of fire! An undeclared war,
Motiveless, strikes at those who contrived
That resonant shell, at ears that have heard
Rejoicings derived, in nights darker by far,
From far greater fires, wells deeper, deep dreams,
Granite, violets, blood, the pureness of dew.

The shell is restored. The orchestra settles.
A baton is raised. Renew what is old!
Make known what is new! From a cello the bow
Draws its hauntingest tone, confiding, profound;
And immured in the bone the marrow responds
To the endless, exploring inventions of sound.

A CHURCH IN BAVARIA

Everything flows
  upward over
    chalk-white walls
      with the ordered freedom
        of a trellised creeper
        wreathed and scrolled
      in a densely choral
anthem of ornament.

Nimble angels
  poise above
    in attitudes,
      huge-limbed prophets
        banner-bearded,
      giant apostles,
      mitred titans
    exemplify
authority,
    their garments ribbed
      in whorls and folds,
        corrugations
          of pearly grace,
        sea-shell volutions
      turned by ages and
    oceans of prayer.

Visions of Paradise
  pivot their rolling
    eyeballs upwards,
      their lips issue
        garlands of praise,
        flexible
      they bend from narrow
    waists, and raise

smooth rounded arms
  with hands adoring
    or holding golden
      instruments,
        long fingers fingering
        tingling harps,
      long trumpets sounding
    triumph unending.

Everything flowers
  in aspiration
    to an imagined
      culmination,
        the athlete spirit's
        endless training
      gives ecstatic
    buoyant lightness,
all aspires as
  shaped and soaring
    white and ring-dove
      grey and gilded
        formal figures
      in a sacred dance.

What does all this
  joyful brilliance
have to do with
  cults obsessed with
    guilt and sin,
      a punishing angry
        vindictive God?
      Where's that hard
    right-angled object
  the Cross, with Victim
blanched by torture,
  dead, with blood?

Here the focal
　　point discloses
　　　　a seated Virgin,
　　her covered head
at a fond angle
in accord with
all this swaying
　　court of images,
　　　looking down
　　　　　benign and gentle
　　　　　at the incredible
　　fact, her Child.

　　Everything sings
　in snowy stillness,
in marble wonder,
　in formal myth,
　　believed because
　　　impossible,
　　　　　believed as only
　　　　a poem can be,
　　the anti-fact
of a holy spore
spreading the Word
　　unsaid before.

　　Everything bends
　　　to re-enact
　　　　the poem lived,
　　　　lived not written,
　　the poem spoken
by Christ, who never
wrote a word,
　saboteur
　　of received ideas
　　　　who rebuilt Rome

with the words he
never wrote;
whether sacred,
whether human,
himself a sunrise
of love enlarged,
of love, enlarged.

A CASUAL ENCOUNTER

(In memory of Cavafy,
1863–1933)

They met, as most these days do,
among streets, not under leaves; at night;
by what is called chance, some think
predestined; in a capital city, latish;
instantly understanding, without words,
without furtiveness, without guilt,
each had been, without calculation, singled out.

Wherever it was they had met,
without introduction, before drifting this way,
beneath lamps hung high, casting
cones of radiance, hazed with pale dust,
a dry pollenous mist that made
each warm surface seem suede, the sense of touch
sang like a harp; the two were alone.

To be private in public added oddness,
out of doors in a city with millions
still awake, with the heard obbligato
of traffic, that resolute drone,
islanding both, their destination
the shadow they stood in. The place
should perhaps be defined.

But need it? Cliff walls of warehouses;
no thoroughfare; at the end a hurrying
river, dragonish; steel gates locked;
emptiness. Whatever they said
was said gently, was not written down,
not recorded. Neither had need
even to know the other one's name.

Nor do you need to know any more
of an hour so far off, so far,
it may be, from what turns you on.
They, with peacefullest smiles at a rare
Befriedigung, parted, breathing the gold-
dusted, denatured air like the pure
air of some alp: nor met ever again.

Is that all? To you it may seem
a commonplace episode. Once was a man
who might not have thought so. To him
(an old photograph hides his neck clamped
in a high stiff white collar, on his pale face
a false-looking moustache) let me dedicate
this moth-winged encounter, to him, to Cavafy himself.

NOTE: I had some correspondence with Cavafy and dedicated
a poem to him. He politely said he was proud of it, but I did not
think well enough of it to reprint it in my *Collected Poems*. Possibly
he might have preferred the present offering.

The old photograph referred to was in a voluminous anthology
of modern Greek poetry which I picked up in Athens in 1930.
Many of the photographs with which it was illustrated were of
soulful and sentimental-looking poetasters. Cavafy's face, photo-
graphed perhaps near the beginning of the century, stood out
among them by its gravity and dignity.

THE AXE IN THE ORCHARD

[In the summer of 1911, when Chekhov had been
dead for seven years, *The Cherry Orchard* was first
performed in London. It was afterwards reported
that at the end of the second act 'signs of dis-
approval were very manifest indeed, and the exodus
from the theatre began'. By the end of the third
act half the audience had departed.]

Nothing was heard but a whisper
Of satin. A notable couple
   Were shown to their places,
Well mated, assured, and upholding
An air of combined high command on
   Their thoroughbred faces.

Sir Something and Lady Someone
(No one remembers them now) —
   She, an Edwardian goddess
With a helmet of maid-brushed hair,
Pearls, and two velvet roses
   Blush-pink in her bodice,

To people she knew bowing slightly,
With the soldierly head of Sir Something
   More rigidly slanted,
His important moustache manifesting
Its wearer a person deferred to,
   Not taken for granted.

Oh, why were they there at the theatre?
They were idle, not curious; a hostess
   Ought to be able,
Lady Someone believed, to show up-to-dateness
And stimulate talk about plays among
   Guests at her table.

Between them and the stage loomed a spectral
Wave-ruling flagship, obscuring
   The sense of the show;
Sir Something and Lady Someone
Never guessed it was doomed and would founder,
   The ship *Status Quo*.

Sir Something's cold glare at his programme
Was like that he turned on from the Bench
   At some rustic offender;
Nothing was heard but his 'Well, now'
(Meaning 'Let's get it over'),
   'Let's see the agenda.'

'Who is this feller? A Russian?
Never heard of him, what? But I bet
   He can't hold a candle
To Arthur Pinero. God help us,
These damn foreign names! Four acts of it, too!
   I call it a scandal.'

Lady Someone said, 'Hush, dear, I know.' She
Was used to his testy complaining.
   Soon nothing was heard
But his mutter, 'Impossible people!
Dull twaddle! Nothing is *happening*!
   The whole thing's absurd!'

Disapproval can circulate quickly;
By the end of Act Two he declared it
   High time to go,
And they rose, with their vertical backbones,
To snub this *new* playwright they'd settled
   Was worthless to know.

But, as was ordained, when the actors
Had gone, when the stage was deserted,
   At the end of the play,

Nothing was heard but the strokes of
The axe in the orchard, the strokes
    of the axe far away.

The strokes of the axe in the orchard
Soon grew louder, unbearably thudding
   By night and by day;
Then nothing was heard but the guns in
The orchards of France. All at once Russia
   Was less far away.

THE PLANES OF BEDFORD SQUARE

Never were the plane trees loftier, leafier,
the planes of Bedford Square,
and of all that summer foliage motionless
not one leaf
had fallen yet, one afternoon
warm in the last world-peace before
the First World War.

At Number Thirty, consulate
of the very last Czar,
before a window on the tall first floor
Baron H., the consul, dreamy
with a Flor de Dindigul cigar,
saw the slow smoke
ghosting an arboreal form.

Tennis was thudding underneath the trees
on grass close-shorn.
A quick racquet flashed
the thump of a return,
and a young voice called the score
as if all was for the best
everywhere, not only on this marked-out lawn.

And all the soaring trees, a tree-of-heaven among them,
wore their enormous shawls of leaves
in full dress, over the court, over
the railed-in shade. Not one leaf,
not one, was yet to fall. On the first floor
was there yet one thought, one
forethought of compulsive and appalling war?

Firbank had started carving hardstone
tesserae to fit his semi-precious prose,
had fondly made a bishop's daughter yearn

'Oh, I could dance for ever
to the valse from *Love Fifteen*!',
foresaw perhaps that she might burn
to ash without one invitation to a ball.

In this well-ordered square the front door yawned
of Number Forty-Four,
and slowly into sunlight sailed
Lady Ottoline, *en grande tenue*, holding herself
as proudly as a rare goose swims;
she was swimming away from the grand and dull,
herself, as ever, too grand to conform.

On her right, the alertest of profiles
fronted the best of brains; her long-boned hand
rested on Bertrand Russell's arm.
On her left, poised on legs
without precedent, Nijinsky himself—
poised as if he could prance for ever
without a thought of any curtain-fall.

Nijinsky, seeing the ballet
of tennis players in white
darting between the tall, theatrical
and sepia-mottled columns of the vaulting trees,
threw out a dancer's arm, and called
in a faun's warm voice
'*Ah, quel décor!*'

The ball slapped into the net. It made the score
a dangerous deuce. A long white ash
dropped from the Baron's cigar. Peace hives
the virus of war. 'Game! And set!'
That moment under the plane trees (*quel décor!*)
was what these lines were cast to recall,
a crystal moment that seemed worth trawling for.

[2]

A VICTORIAN ALBUM

Matriarch, admiral, pert-faced boy,
chlorotic virgin, plethoric bon-vivant,
London dandy, High Church dean or don, two
reposeful sisters (white skins never shown
to the sun, white hands that need never work).

Braid and brocade and broadcloth, made to last;
shrill watered-silk over stiff corsetry;
frock-coats, crinolines, aiglets, galloons, and lace;
costly simplicity; upright backs
against straight-backed chairs; a sword, a Bible, a fan.

Characters! Each (against tasselled drapes,
plaster balusters, pedestals) looked at the lens
with that look on which no sun could ever set,
with a poise derived from pride of birth,
race, class, property, privilege, place.

White, Protestant, English or Scottish,
all these were WE, the rest of the world being THEY —
the low-born or ill-bred, the new rich, the always-
with-us poor; heathens; and foreigners who
from Dover, when clear, could almost be seen to begin.

Turn the page, with your anti-imperial hand.
Who has got among us now? Who on earth
is this? A mahogany-skinned and proud
young Muslim, smiling, handsome, assured.
Thanks to him, I am here to write this today.

That's Osman, who in the Mutiny saved
my grandfather's life, I suppose because
he thought it worth saving. There he stands
great among grandparents, grand among great-
uncles and aunts, he who put friendship first.

NO IDENTITY

Against the name of the place we mean to move to
The guidebook bleakly rules *No identity*:
What Doctor Pevsner means is absence of ancient
Or markworthy buildings.
                         What he implies
Is a shallowly-rooted community, a huddlement
Of not very settled commuters, interspersed with retired
Couples, tending to dwindle to widows,
Little communal sense or parish pride,
And the usual private or commonplace fears
Like that of being moved to some distant branch
Of one's place of work, or of cold old age.

But if a triumphal arch were to welcome us
What better inscription than this, *No identity*?
We are not the sort who wish to reflect prestige
From a rare environment. By possessing antiques
Or using the newest things we feel no need
To reinforce our own identity; at our age
That seems unambiguous enough.
                               My need
As a poet (not every poet's) is this —
To be immersed in a neutral solution, which
Alone provides an interim, until through the grey
Expectant film invisible writing comes clean.

No identity can be a desirable thing:
To have a face with features noticed less
Than one's range of expression, so that photographed
It never looks twice the same, and people say
'But that's not you!'
                      One would like to reply:
'No, that's not me, because I'm incapable
Of starting the very least personality cult.

I have freed myself at last from being me;
Don't think of me as chameleon or actor; if I take
Protective colouring, it is that I mean to be
A kind of medium, free to enjoy, well, *no identity*.'

ANONYMA

Anxiety dream: late at the
station, train at the
platform, doors all finally
slamming, guard at the
ready, how can I possibly — ?
Exacerbating delay with
ticket, and train about to,
about to, about to
move — but out of it
a hand is waving, I see the smiling
face of Anonyma. All will be well now,
on the train with her;
train leaving.

The train has taken me, taken me
straight out of the dream,
filled with well-being by
reunion with Anonyma.
Waking I remember
she died thirty years ago;
serene, am not awake enough
to feel surprise at
her being alive still.
I see she's immortal.
After thirty years to enter
the dream of a survivor
creatively!

In after years, in some other country,
perhaps I too may smile
welcome in the troubled
sleep of a doubter;
on the cold forehead of solitude
lay four fingers of warmth;

give comfort by my company
to some lone fighter;
with this dead hand signal
lively understanding. Just as
she did me, I might hearten someone.
Such a chain-reaction
might have no ending.

THEATRE OF DREAMS

In a cool element of unvarying
shadowless dreamlight,
in a theatre of sinister caprice,
all stage and no audience,
it is here you must act —
to this you have been brought
by lying down under
a sheet of silence, under
a blanket of darkness.

It is a place without reason or logic,
without clock or calendar,
where the dead may be met living
and you may with intense pleasure
enjoy familiarity with strangers,
a place of unforeseeable situations
in which your part is determined
by two dramatists of genius,
collaborators, Fear and Desire.

Imagine a play without rehearsals,
the acting impromptu,
long planned, but not put in writing,
a play given one performance
only, in fact only for you.
It's not just entertainment:
the two dramatists, you understand,
are dangerous prisoners, their plays
a substitute for liberation.

TENSION AT SUNSET

A touch of gigantism
is distorting the landscape,
and this on a still day,
cloudless, painted on porcelain.

Huge low-slung spotlight
angled from emptiness, the sun
colours the corals in a hawthorn hedge
and the damson colonies of sloes.

The sunflowers have gone out;
their vertical green pipes
now hold up discs of monochrome mosaic;
these discs look monstrous in the clean air,
itself abnormal in a dirtied world.

The level glare is caught
in the burning glass of a shut
window miles away. One cannot bear
to look at it, nor could one look out of it.

Along the bare hillside
the shadow of a tree,
of one small tree,
is a hundred times its length;
its elastic shadow has no breaking-point.
At this moment exaggeration
is seen to be infinite.

This might be the moment,
the right moment for a showdown,
for something postponed
to be made to happen;

but all the long shadows are merging
into one shadow,
into a restless night,
into an unresolved problem
waiting for daylight
to ring its alarm.

[*3*]

STONES OF ARGYLL

Clans, claymores, cackle about battles,
Jacobites, Covenanters, noisy Knox,
that tall thin nympho Queen of Scots —
all those, to a petrologist, are trash,
newspaper stuff. Newspapers are used
for lighting fires or wrapping fish.

You pick up scraps of gossip out of books:
that's history. Prehistory for me!
Don't misunderstand me if I say 'That's gneiss,'
I'm looking at 300 million years,
at how the world was made. Stones
are what I mean by concrete poetry.

The tide receding from this beach
makes every stone fresher than paint —
cake-like conglomerate, black basalt,
pink granite, purplish andesite,
quartzite, felsite. Gorgeous most
these reddish jaspers with their soapy feel.

FIVE WILD ORCHIDS

['I hunted curious flowers in rapture and mut-
tered thoughts in their praise.'

John Clare]

We won't pick nor let a camera see
these perfect five,
nor tell a single person where they are.

I see their tint and detailed singularity
delineated by a fine, devoted hand
some sunlit sheep-bell afternoon, two centuries ago.

Next year they may increase
or not, along this untouched slope in June,
this unfrequented mild escarpment.

Unlikely we'll be here again
to see the silk-
winged inflorescence on new stems.

We've interrupted their rarity.
With rapture, with praise, with deference
we back away, muttering.

IN A CATHEDRAL TOWN

Nothing unusual in the irritable shoving
of one-way traffic through the town
on this technological morning.

Yes, something unusual — a woman
alone on the pavement, in a faded coat,
perhaps forty, with uncombed hair.

She might have been unnoticed,
but raising and lowering a short stick
points repeatedly at a shop opposite.

Ignoring the traffic and passers-by,
aiming her accusing stick, she mutters
incantations, curses.

She has been seen by the shop manager;
with one glossy saleswoman he stares
through plate glass, over the traffic.

Both wear a look of contemptuous amusement,
of superior tolerance, but fail to hide
annoyance and uneasiness at her persistence.

There's no knowing what has provoked her,
nor how long she has been aiming, aiming,
nor whether her manoeuvres are effective.

As if solitude has distilled it,
the witch looks wildly alone with her venom,
erect, independent, a pythoness.

Computers, commuters, cathedral committees
have missed out this other technician
and the assured gestures of primitive magic.

The plate glass may shatter,
the shop fail, the manager collapse,
the saleswoman miscarry.

YOUR HEART AND THE MOON

If, when you gaze at the moon,
about which so many have raved,
your susceptible heart gives a thump,
this proves that a dull desert craved
by yet-to-be far-flung bores
can excite a transplantable pump.
                              [1968]

TO THE MOON AND BACK

countdown   takeoff
moonprints   rockbox
splashdown   claptrap

THE RED FAULT LAMP

The red fault lamp
in the zero reset push-button
is lit on one axis, look,
and it still stays lit
after fault resetting, after checking
it still stays lit:
where do we go from here?

Another thing I don't know
is where should the x and y
oscilloscope input leads be connected
if a check is needed
of the optics signal waveform?
Look at the red fault lamp,
it still stays lit.

Somewhere something is wrong,
as it usually is;
after checking, after resetting
who would ever have thought
the mean little red fault lamp
would still stay lit?
My third question: no answer.

From back there no answer,
nor likely to be now we're this far out
with the moon small as a nut.
Yes, there goes the tiny moon now,
take one last look at it.
And here *we* go, three nuts in space,
with our red fault lamp still lit.

THEY

Do you think about them at all? They
either don't think at all, or think nothing,
or think vaguely of you. They
think what's good to be done or is done well
is only so if done by their own set.

You've been and have done what you could
by being yourself, not one of a set. They
in their zipped-up self-importance
hear your name (they do just hear your name)
condescendingly. Some even praise you.

You once made the mistake you could only
make once, of being young; and so provoked
in them (as they then were) some envy.
Life's motor is habit, so they went on
calling you young till you were bent like a boomerang.

They've stayed unchanged while the usual process
was cutting deep glyphs in your withering face,
but when your hair turned white in a single
decade, they saw it was high time
to disregard you and write you off as stale buns.

As you have for some time built up
what you could against the ravening ebb-tide
with what skill you had and as chance allowed,
and since what you built has form
and is still added to, it's not unknown. They

seeing it not unknown can't quite ignore it. Now,
if they praise, they praise you for what
you're not, or for what they allege you
to have once been. With quaint smugness
they applaud their false image of you.

Oddly supposing some judgment needed from them
yet always flummoxed by the imaginative,
or prophetic, or creatively marginal,
they compare it to what they fall for —
the trivial, the trendy, the ephemeral.

If you do happen to waffle on to a great age
they'll allow you a slight curiosity-value
as a survival of a species almost extinct;
they'll patronize you with a show of false esteem,
unaware that you seldom read or hear what they say.

It's plain that by deviating in your own way
you've made what you have. You've made it
clear, durable, pointed as a cluster of crystals. They,
they have grown nothing but a great goitre
of mediocrity — not only unsightly, it's incurable.

CONTEMPORARIES

N., A DIDACTIC JOURNALIST

N. has no time for God; devout
self-worship keeps him quite content.
O God, if able to believe in N.,
You're proved omnipotent.

MRS CANUTE, A REFORMER

Oh for my non-permissive youth!
I shall not rest, as I had planned,
till I have built Tabusalem
In England's mad, unbuttoned land.

POSITIVE

['Positive is the perfection of coxcomb,
he is then come to his full growth.'
George Savile, Marquess of Halifax, 1633–95]

His self-esteem has outrun calculation:
you'd make the biggest fortune ever known
if you could buy him at your valuation —
and sell him at his own.

[4]

BUREAUCRATIC NEGATIVES

[White South Africans oddly describe themselves
as 'Europeans' and black South Africans as 'non-
Europeans'. 'If anybody asks me what country I
come from,' said a black South African, 'I shall
have to say "Non-Europe".' When he asked for a
passport he met with a flat refusal. He was told
he could have an 'exit permit', entitling him to
leave the country but not to return to it.]

What's language for?
I'll tell you what:
it's not to call us what we are
but tell us what we're not.

You can't have a passport,
you're not a non-black:
this permit to go is a
non-permit to come back.

The dead are non-living,
the hungry non-fed:
don't think because you're non-unconscious
that you're alive —you're non-dead.

PASSED BY THE CENSOR

'The Publications Control
Board has decided to allow
South Africans to put ice-
cubes made in the shape of
female nude dolls into their
drinks. Disclosing this infor-
mation at a women's gather-
ing this week, a member of
the Board, Mrs J. P. Theron,
said it had been decided to
allow the dolly ice-cubes
because they melted so
quickly in the liquor.

The Board was not nar-
row-minded, said Mrs
Theron.'—*Cape Times*.

What a corrupting new device!
But in this case my ruling is
　　Our rules need not be rigid:
These topless girls are bottomless,
And though they give one melting looks
　　They're pure. What's more, they're frigid.

WHITE GLOVES

Reading some Russian novel
    far on a Transvaal steppe,
blue hills near in the clean sky's lens
    and Russia brought quite as near
in the focus of prose, the place I was in
    and was not were strangely merged.

Straight as a caryatid
    a brown girl held on her head
a brown girl's burden of white things washed
    for whites, of whom I was one:
she knew she was graceful, I knew
    her life was the life of a serf.

Now, with half a century gone,
    a letter that comes from those parts
shows by its turn and tone of phrase
    it comes from a Tolstoi-time,
from a sun-dried Russia where even now
    the serfs have not yet been freed.

A terrace in lilied shade,
    ice clinks in glasses there,
white gloves disguise black hands that offer
    a tray—untouchable hands.
Cars race to a feast. On the burning veld
    slow peasants stand apart.

The scene dissolves to Kazan:
    the snowy versts race past,
wrapped snug in furs we chatter in French
    as with clinking harness-bells
we drive to a feast. On the frozen road
    slow peasants step aside.

Some other caryatid
  no doubt, after all these years,
barefoot and slow, with patient steps
  in the place I knew upholds
with her strength what has to be done:
  the serfs are not yet freed.

Not of them the letter brings news
  but of a picnic, a bride,
white bride of the son of a millionaire,
  and of pleasures bought. It implies
that a usual social round
  runs on its inbuilt power,

runs by itself, by right;
  will last; must drive, not walk.
Alone and apart, more alone and apart
  it floats, floats high, that world
with the tinted oiliness
  of a bubble's tensile skin:

but inside the bubble a serf,
  black serf, peels off his gloves,
white gloves. With naked hands
  he opens a door FOR WHITES ALONE
and salutes in a mirror the self
  he is destined at last to meet.

[5]

THE GURU

The father figures lie in broken pieces,
broken eggshells
out of which we had to break away.
The pedestals they stood on
serve as paving stones.

Old men! We talk to them
but they're not listening,
they're looking inwards,
listening to the past.

Old men! Each a city in himself,
he listens to the traffic that he knows,
his arteries are memories,
every corpuscle a human face.

Old men! They know you're free,
they're longing to control you,
they judge you,
they condemn you,
they're longing to reform you.

And yet among them is the guru.
You can recognize the guru:
he respects you,
he accepts you.

Purged of conceit
and far beyond resentment,
he won't condemn us.
How can he,
when he knows in each of us
has been, is, or may be
the seed of every other?

When we don't know what we're doing
but think we know,
the guru lays his patience as a path
for us to walk on
if we want to.

He learns by teaching,
and calmly he can view
among his million other selves
the self that's you.

ANOTHER OLD MAN

'On my ancestor's tomb
this epitaph's cut:
HE WAS UPRIGHT, MODEST, AND AFFABLE.
That's possible, but
let my epitaph say:

SOMETIMES THINKING ALOUD
HE WENT HIS OWN WAY.
HE WAS JOKY BY NATURE,
SAD, SCEPTICAL, PROUD.
WHAT HE NEVER WOULD FOLLOW,
OR LEAD, WAS A CROWD.'

AT A MEMORIAL SERVICE

All here are formalists.
In the cruciform church
all stand facing east. All kneel.
Each muffles his faith, or no faith,
in old clean robes of prayer.
All attend, as words model
an image of a man they remember.
Here and there in a grey head
remembrance now stings
disused lachrymal ducts.

As a death brings them back to
their inherited cult
those decent grey heads,
respectful, respected,
conforming, are calmed.
One man less, they're estranged
that much more from the angry
menace outside,
the mad new Establishment
of loud disrespect.

As they rise to intone
an articulate hymn,
beneath it, in unison,
breathes a vast sighing
out of old tribal times:
migrant birds over oceans
rush, not knowing why,
their consensus of confidence
one soft brush touching
danger, day, and the dark.

PUT UP TO BE SHOT AT

Your life is a target
exposed to a marksman
who shoots when he feels like it.

There's no doubt who he is,
and it's no good supposing
anything can stop him.
When you think him asleep, he may
take aim again, casually
nicking an outer.

After years of immunity
you may end up as full of
holes as a colander.

Or even now one shot may
punch through the heart of you
a peephole at infinity.

But would you wish to be
never at all shot at?
Isn't that unthinkable?

SLEEPING ALONE

Needing night's amnesia
she folds the sheet about her shoulder
and the dark across her eyes,
but the sinking pillow is a trap,
leaves her utterly alone,
unprotected, to her dreams.

Though a folded wing of hair
guards her eyelids, though a guarding
arm is round her, there she dreams
dreaded dreams which resurrect the dead:
courage cannot ever make her
stronger than those revenants.

DEATH OF A HEDGE-SPARROW

This afternoon it stood alone
Beside me, showed no fear,
Resting its head between its wings.
After an hour it moved, it fell,
Under a tower of leaves
Careened, and there it lay.

There as it lay, its thin,
Its thorn-fine claws
Encircled emptiness;
Its dew-bright eyes began
To blur. Its pin-point beak
Drank three quick sips of air.

Then it half seemed to sigh,
Stretched with (too faint to hear)
One last, fan-opening whirr
To full extent both wings,
In flight from life;
They slowly closed.
It shivered once; lay still.

To mind there sprang
A Roman phrase, *Ubi humilitas,*
Ibi majestas. Great marble word
For an almost weightless corpse!
My little pang was not excess
Of sentiment, it was proportionate
(Sole witness, I affirm) to what I saw.

NOW

I

Lonely old woman, her husband died
on some useless alp.
Lonely old woman, widow
of a lost civilization.

A prisoner of habit, at home
she has lived on and on, inside a dream
of her safe early years
in a lost civilization.

This once quiet by-road's now a by-pass.
Her well-built house stands well back
half hidden by trees,
and not yet for sale.

'Rare opportunity,'
some agent will announce,
'gracious detached
character residence of older type,
might suit institution, requires
some modernization,'
having been planned for
a lost civilization.

Prodding and peeping in this acre of jungle,
once a garden, a modernizer
may break his leg, snared
by a rusty croquet-hoop
or the lead rim of a half buried
ornamental cistern.
There's no gardener now.

Like the house its owners
were gracious, detached,
thought it wiser not to love
one's neighbour as oneself,
wisest
to be only upon nodding terms.

As clear as an inscription
their thoughts could be read:

> *Presuming on propinquity*
> *neighbours might show themselves,*
> *might show curiosity,*
> *or, by asking questions,*
> *familiarity.*
>
> *How appalling*
> *if they were to speak*
> *about themselves!*
> *They might try and impress one,*
> *or, absurdly, pretend*
> *one couldn't impress them —*
> *as if one would ever bother*
> *to make the attempt!*
>
> *I suppose if appealed to*
> *in some crisis*
> *one might be driven,*
> *yes, driven by imprudence,*
> *to play the Samaritan.*

2

Under the heavier and heavier alluvium of noise
deafness has silted up and sealed the house.
In unremembered, as if Etruscan, painted rooms
rare and hand-made undiscovered things are waiting,

finely made to last, things handed down
and kept with the respectful care of those
accustomed to good things—things touched and seen
almost as if animate, things heartfelt.

To have assets or have food to eat
was once inseparable from thanks; wastefulness
by rich or poor, so it was taught,
was wrong; but avarice was despised.
Now by-pass lives are caught up in a complex
of invented needs that money-suckers boost
for quantities of trash, fallible,
expendable, much of it indestructible.

First thing in the morning, drawing back
threadbare curtains to light her loveless days,
habit makes her note the night's additions
to the day's, to every day's, disjections:
over her straggled hedge bottles and cartons fly,
cans, another broken mattress, one more white
up-ended broken stove, and nameless things,
conglomerating a malignant growth.

3

'Horner has died, who used to put things right
and keep things straight for me, and keep things clean,
and make things grow. He fought for tidiness
against the weather, gales, weeds, pests.
"Mustn't let Nature have her way," he said.
He knew that gardening is an art. I used to think
he seemed in the garden like a worshipper,
bowed down and kneeling all those devoted years.

'Now Mrs Horner's gone. Twice the corner wall
of Mrs Horner's cottage quite collapsed
under the impact of a ten-wheeled lorry.

Neither time was Mrs Horner, who did everything
for me, there in the room. So fortunate!
"It would be tempting Providence," she said,
"to use that room again." After repairs
she always kept it locked, and empty too.

'In this house now I only use two rooms.
Thanks to my deafness, I don't hear them now,
those dreadful lorries, like warehouses going by,
and motor-bicycles, so fast, the wild young men
fly past with streaming hanks of hair
jerking back in the wind like snakes,
and frantic fringes on their leather coats —
off to their coven, I fancy, on some blasted heath.'

4

'As for me, I never mope.
I dodge self-pity like the plague.
Hope? A drug I'm now immune to.
I expect to finish here, alone.
If I collapse, am found, and driven away,
what good would that do? None.

'I'm light as a feather now,
dry papery skin, and like my mother
I'm small-boned.
I can imagine after a long delay
forcible entry, and what was me on the floor
like a discarded summer travelling-coat,

'or like a dried-up butterfly
(butterflies never learn that the finest fidgeting
continued and continued even all summer long
can never make that wall of solid air,
a sheet of glass, a sudden
change to freedom),

'or like the sloughed skin of a snake
(I hope I may say non-poisonous).
Lying there, I'll be proved less durable
than my Tudor spoon, my Hilliard,
or my melon-slice of jade.
Exquisite, isn't it?

'One hope I have, that these few pretty things
inherited or acquired, outlasting me,
may be cherished for what they are
more than for what they'd fetch.
Who, you may ask, is to inherit them?
Leaving the world, I leave them to the world.'